THE KENNEDY FAMILY ALBUM

RUNNING PRESS
PHILADELPHIA · LONDON

THE KENNEDY FAMILY ALBUM

LINDA CORLEY

PHOTOGRAPHS BY BOB DAVIDOFF

9   8   7   6   5   4   3   2   1

Digit on the right indicates the number of this printing

Library of Congress Control Number: 2008926624

ISBN 978-1-56025-923-7

Cover design by Bill Jones

Interior design by Lorie Pagnozzi

Edited by Jennifer Kasius

Typography: Mrs Eaves, and Gill Sans

Running Press Book Publishers

2300 Chestnut Street

Philadelphia, PA 19103-4371

Visit us on the web!

www.runningpress.com

For my Bobby, I will love you forever and always. And for our sons, Kenneth, Michael, and Daryl, who for years shot side by side with their father and are following in his footsteps. And finally to Linda Corley, for accomplishing and finishing what Bobby dreamed of doing for so many years.

I love you all very much,
BABE DAVIDOFF

TABLE OF CONTENTS

ACKNOWLEDGMENTS

A special thank you to:

Senator Edward "Ted" Kennedy for his friendship

Gloria Mosch for her years of dedication to all the Davidoff family

Harry Elson, for inspiring Bobby many years ago to "do a book"

Tony Mark and Lucien Carter in Senator Ted Kennedy's office for all their help

Geir Lilleeng, C. J., and Landon for their love and support

Alice Bernard for her friendship and guidance

The *Palm Beach Post* for opening up their archives

Leo Racine and Cynthia Ray Stone for sharing their recollections of working with
the Kennedy Family

Linda Konner and Anita Diggs for their belief in the project, and to Jennifer Kasius for
making it a reality.

And finally to Lisa Emalfarb, for making the introduction to Bob Davidoff, for if it wasn't for
that magic moment, this book wouldn't have been possible.

—LINDA CORLEY AND BABE DAVIDOFF

FOREWORD

Bob Davidoff was a magnificent photographer and a loyal friend. His remarkable personality

and charming sense of humor had us all smiling whenever he aimed his camera our way. For

me, his legacy will live on in the wonderful photographs he took of our family over the years and

the collection of prints he generously donated to the John F. Kennedy Presidential Library in

Boston. His warmth and thoughtfulness will be greatly missed by all of us in the Kennedy family

and by all those who knew and loved him as we did and were awed by his talent with a camera.

—SENATOR EDWARD M. KENNEDY

THE KENNEDY FAMILY ALBUM

THE WHITE HOUSE

WASHINGTON

May 6, 1963

Dear Mr. Davidoff:

Mrs. Kennedy has asked me to write to thank you for your courtesy in giving her the photographs which you took of her and her family in Palm Beach.

I am enclosing the large photograph which you sent, with her signature.

With every good wish, I am

Sincerely yours,

Pamela Turnure
Press Secretary
to Mrs. Kennedy

Mr. Bob Davidoff
Bob Davidoff Studios
121 Bradley Place
Palm Beach, Florida

THE KENNEDYS OF PALM BEACH

Letter to Bob from the White House.

PALM BEACH IN THE WINTER AND HYANNIS PORT IN THE SUMMER, TWO TOWNS NORTH AND SOUTH THAT SERVED AS VACATION DESTINATIONS FOR THE KENNEDY FAMILY. THESE SPECIAL PLACES ARE WHERE THE KENNEDYS TOOK TIME TOGETHER TO SAIL, GOLF, PLAY TOUCH FOOTBALL, AND FORM THEIR FAMILY BONDS. While other families took mere vacations, the extended Kennedy family met during holidays and summer breaks at one of these two family homes to partake in a seasonal tribal ritual. Here they enjoyed each other's company, heartily engaged in sports, and when tragedy struck found solace from the outside world.

The Kennedy estate in Palm Beach

While Hyannis Port in Cape Cod was the Kennedy family's summer home, consisting of several houses that would serve as the backdrop for large and informal Kennedy gatherings for years to come, the Palm Beach estate was no less important. It was here that the Kennedy clan achieved social standing among the great dynasties of Palm Beach. The once working-class Irish American family from Boston was finally hob-nobbing with the DuPonts, the Posts, and the Duke and Duchess of Windsor.

It was during the Palm Beach social season of 1959 that photographer Bob Davidoff first met Rose Kennedy. At the time, Davidoff worked for United Press International and had gained a solid reputation for recording all of the glittery comings and goings of Palm Beach society. One night Davidoff, covering an opening at the Royal Poinciana Playhouse, snapped a few photos of Rose that would appear in the Palm Beach Daily News.

When the article appeared the following day, Rose was immediately impressed by his photos and encouraged her social secretary to find the photographer's home phone number so she could tell him in person. His wife, Babe, answered the phone, and when the tiny voice punctuated with a heavy Boston accent stated it was Rose Kennedy, Babe was sure it was a prank call and hung up.

In the months to come, Davidoff would take many society photos of Rose and, as always, made sure that only the most flattering shots would get into the hands of the society papers. It was his talent as a photographer, combined with his respectful attitude, that earned him entrée into the private world of the great American family in the decades that followed.

Davidoff slowly became a fixture at the Palm Beach home as well as a confidant and friend of Rose. Over the years Davidoff would record the sun-filled side of Camelot as the president and his young family made their way south from Washington for rest and relaxation. He would capture many of the milestone moments of the presidency along with the famous faces that were associated with the Kennedy administration. After the White House era, Davidoff continued his relationship with the extended family, including with the glamorous Jackie while she vacationed in Palm Beach with her second husband, Aristotle Onassis. Eventually Davidoff ventured off the island on occasion to take pictures of the third generation of Kennedys as they enjoyed sleigh rides together in Sun Valley, Idaho, or maneuvered sailboats through rough seas off Cape Cod.

An aerial view of the "Winter White House" in 1985.

For decades Davidoff's pictures not only appeared in top newspapers and magazines across the country, but because of the often playful nature of his images, many rare and unpublished photos landed in personal scrapbooks of the Kennedys and are still treasured by family members today.

Jackie Kennedy once remarked to Davidoff as they took a stroll down the beach outside the Kennedys' Florida home, "The photographs [that you've] taken during the presidential years are valued keepsakes for me. I look through them now and remember [such things as] Caroline standing up on a chair in a hamburger restaurant . . . and saying, 'My daddy's the president of the United States!'"

The young Bob Davidoff

Rose Kennedy with grandson John Jr.
at St. Edwards, March 11, 1973.

President Kennedy peeking
out the front door of the
Florida Kennedy home,
April 1963.

Jackie walking up the pier at Hyannis Port, September 1975.

A happy Ted Jr. waves to the camera alongside his mother, Joan, father, Senator Edward Kennedy, and sister Kara, outside the Kennedy home in Palm Beach, December 1969.

The Shriver family posing for a Christmas card photo, November 26, 1972. Clockwise from front: Mark, Maria, Sargent, Anthony, Robert, Timothy and Eunice (center).

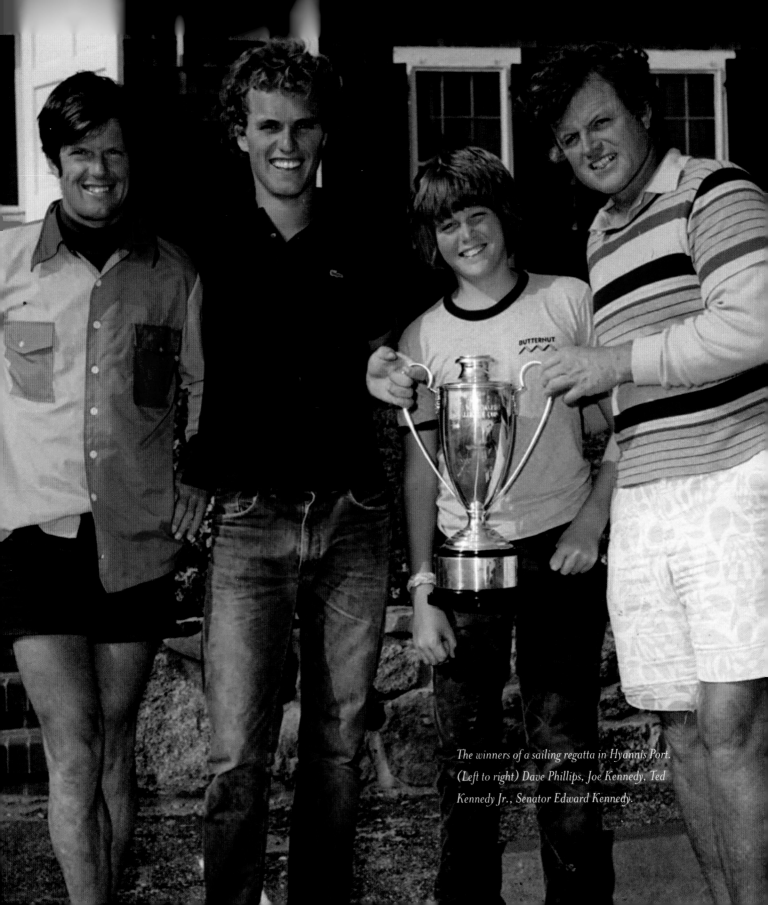

*The winners of a sailing regatta in Hyannis Port.
(Left to right) Dave Phillips, Joe Kennedy, Ted
Kennedy Jr., Senator Edward Kennedy.*

Senator and Mrs. Edward Kennedy on their way to Christmas service in Palm Beach, December 25, 1964.

Victoria Lawford with her mother, Pat, March 21, 1975.

Sargent and Eunice Shriver on Christmas Day in Palm Beach, 1975.

Ted Kennedy and clan in Sun Valley, Idaho, January 1976.

Rose Kennedy (seated) at the Red Cross Ball at the Breakers, January 1976.

CHAPTER ONE

THE ROSE OF PALM BEACH

R OSE KENNEDY WAS INTRODUCED TO PALM BEACH IN 1911. AT THE AGE TWENTY-ONE, SHE WAS TAKEN DOWN SOUTH FOR VISITS TO THE GREAT RESORT TOWN BY HER FATHER, JOHN "HONEY FITZ" FITZGERALD, THE MAYOR OF BOSTON. As a young woman she fell in love with the island, its grand hotels and renowned high society. Palm Beach was a place of formality, and Rose enjoyed all of its elegant splendor. Her wonderful memories prompted her to introduce her husband, Joseph P. Kennedy, to the island in the twenties, and in 1933 he would purchase the Mizner estate at 1095 North Ocean Blvd.

Although originally called "La Guerida," the house would become known to the world as the "Winter White House." In the early nineties it was dubbed the "Kennedy Compound." But to the Kennedy family, it was simply referred to as "The Beach House."

Davidoff remembered the low-key air surrounding the estate. "There were certainly grander homes on the island. I suppose you could even describe their home as plain. This was the place the Kennedys came to relax and kick their shoes off. With the number of family members that came in and out over the years, the interior was designed to hold up to wear and tear . . . not to impress."

Though the estate did not have air conditioning or heat, the home was often described as comfortable and casual. With seven bedrooms, tennis court, large swimming pool, and a stretch of private beach, the house was ideal for the vacationing Kennedys.

It was here on the backyard lawn that John F. Kennedy wrote *Profiles in Courage*; out on the pool terrace was the spot where he would announce his first cabinet. During the early sixties neighbors would remember him holding impromptu press conferences at the front door of the estate. In 1974 this wooden door would be recognized as a historic landmark.

In the early years, long before the presidency, the entire family descended from their main home in Brookline,

Rose Kennedy, Ambassador Joseph Kennedy, Ann Gargan (niece) and John Tumulty (behind Ambassador Kennedy) (other two unidentified) at the Great Lady Ball, The Everglades Club, Palm Beach, Florida, March 16, 1961.

Massachusetts, usually around the holidays of Christmas and Easter. Eventually, as the children grew older, Rose would spend the entire social season in Palm Beach, which lasted from December through March.

In later years she would enjoy her solitude in the Palm Beach home and her daily long walks on the beach. The peace was disrupted around the holidays when her children would continue the pilgrimage south with a multitude of their children in tow.

"Rose told me that these years were her favorite time of life," Davidoff recalled. "She could enjoy her children's accomplishments, revel in being a grandmother, and have time off from the responsibilities of childrearing to reminisce about the wondrous events of so many years ago."

PALM BEACH SOCIETY

The right clothes, the right address, and of course entreé to the right parties were all important to Rose Kennedy. In the fifties being an Irish American from Boston was not always a welcome invitation to blue-blood enclaves like the Everglades Club and the Bath and Tennis Club. Rose had some work to do in order to be accepted, and being the mother of senators, congressmen, and the president of United States certainly expedited her initiation into the private and exclusive Palm Beach circles.

But despite her wealth and social standing, Rose remained down-to-earth and approachable. Davidoff described her as "a spunky woman with a very youthful air." She was known to walk miles in the rain, play hours of golf despite the heat, and swim endless laps in the pool. Davidoff once heard through the grapevine that when no one was at home, she preferred to swim without a swimsuit.

"That was Rose. She did what she wanted," said Davidoff, "She may have been opinionated, but she wasn't stubborn. Despite her earthy quality, she was always a lady. You couldn't help but respect her."

The Duchess of Windsor, Winston Guest and Rose Kennedy at the Polo Ball, March 16, 1961.

Rose with Palm Beach friends boarding a private plane for a quick trip to the Bahamas.

{*T h e   K e n n e d y   F a m i l y   A l b u m*}

There is a local legend that describes a Kennedy tea at the Winter White House. One of Palm Beach's grandes dames was trying to get out of the narrow driveway after the event but quickly became stuck due the line of cars blocking the area. Rose immediately walked out into the street and began directing traffic. All dressed up in high heels and a designer dress, Rose assumed the role of a traffic cop as easily as she played the role of one of America's best known matriarchs.

Morton Downey, Mary Sanford and Rose Kennedy at a party hosted by Palm Beach socialite Brownie McLean, November 23, 1979.

*George Hamilton and Rose
Kennedy at the Henry Flagler
Museum, January 17, 1974.*

THE FASHION QUEEN

Davidoff recalled Rose Kennedy's penchant for fine clothes. Her drive to maintain equal status with the society matrons of Palm Beach swept her away to Paris at least once a year to view the latest designer collections. She went as far as learning French so that she could converse with the up-and-coming couturiers of the day. Rose wanted to immerse herself in the language on a daily basis, so she hired a French secretary who also worked diligently on softening her Boston accent when she spoke the delicate language. "Rose would come back from Paris all excited and wanted me to take portraits of her in a few ensembles she brought back," said Davidoff. "She would even try her French on me during the photo sessions, but of course I couldn't understand a damn thing she was saying!"

*Rose Kennedy, Joseph and Estée Lauder at
the Red Cross Ball, January 1976.*

*Dressed in a mantilla, Rose attends the Palm Beach
gallery with the Marquis de Larrain and good friend Mary
Sanford, March 1977.*

Mary Sanford, Senator Edward Kennedy and Rose Kennedy at the Red Cross Ball, January, 1972.

Davidoff always knew when the social season was approaching because he would get a call from Rose. Davidoff said because of his years among the social set of Palm Beach, Rose would seek his advice. "She would ask me about who was going to which party, what I thought she should wear and, if need be, background information about the people who were hosting a particular party."

Because of her role as the mother of the president of the United States, Rose took her appearance very seriously. She was fiercely concerned about making the right impression. "It was important," said Davidoff, "especially when you were seated next to international fashion leaders like the Duchess of Windsor or C. Z. Guest."

Rose Kennedy at the Red Cross Ball, January 1966.

Stayton Addison, manager of the Breakers Hotel, Pat Lawford, Rose Kennedy and Senator Edward Kennedy
at an Anti-Defamation League event, February 7, 1980.

Rose Kennedy and Mrs. Ordway at the Palm Beach Playhouse Kiwanis benefit starring Victor Borge, 1962.

Rose and her good friend Mary Sanford listening to Lowell Guinness speak at the Henry Flagler Museum during the early sixties.

Rose on the beach behind her home in Palm Beach in 1977. Still fit and trim in her eighties, Rose was adamant about keeping in shape. Her daily routine included long walks to the north end of the island, rain or shine. An avid golfer, she would play nine holes every day at the Palm Beach Country Club until her eyesight became so poor that she had trouble seeing the ball. Although she became quite an accomplished golfer over the years, she never kept score.

Rose, just back from Paris, models one of her favorite purchases. Her dressmaker in Palm Beach said Rose was very particular about her clothes, in fact she insisted that her dresses be double lined so that in the event a breeze picked the dress up, the inside of the garment would be identical to the outside.

A WOMAN OF FAITH
AND CHARITY

IF EITHER MAN OR WOMAN WOULD REALIZE THAT
THE FULL POWER OF PERSONAL BEAUTY, IT MUST
BE BY CHERISHING NOBLE THOUGHTS AND HOPES
AND PURPOSES; BY HAVING SOMETHING TO DO
AND SOMETHING TO LIVE FOR THAT IS WORTHY
OF HUMANITY, AND WHICH, BY EXPANDING AND
SYMMETRY TO THE BODY WHICH CONTAINS IT.

—ROSE KENNEDY

Although the glamorous balls in the name of charity
were a pleasurable pastime for the social set of Palm
Beach, for Rose charity went beyond satin gowns and
ballroom slippers. Charity undoubtedly meant public
service, a belief she tried to instill in her children and
grandchildren for years to come. The Special Olympics,
founded by her daughter Eunice, was an organization
close to Rose's heart. She would always be one of the
first volunteers to arrive at an event and one of the last
to leave.

*Rose, a deeply devoted Catholic,
sometimes attended mass as often as
twice a day. Many close to her, including
her secretary Cynthia Stone Ray, felt it
was her faith that kept her going through
all the tragedies during her lifetime.*

"We would have long talks on the phone about the importance of giving back,"
recalled Davidoff. "Rose was always encouraging her children to tithe more diligently,
get more involved in social causes. The biblical quote 'to whom much is given, much will
be required' was a favorite of Rose's. It is no doubt President Kennedy would use that
line in one of his speeches. She was always a great example to her family because she was
a woman of great faith and compassion."

After her daughter Eunice had founded the Special Olympics in 1968, Rose was always ready to give a helping hand. Here at a local competition in West Palm Beach, Rose lends her support as she shows great interest in the children and their accomplishments. Bob recalls she was always the first to arrive and often one of the last to leave the events.

Rose Kennedy mailing the first letter to be addressed with a Special Olympics stamp from her home in Palm Beach, Florida, January 1968.

Rose Kennedy attends the Special Olympics in
West Palm Beach, March 14, 1977.

THE GRAND MATRIARCH

As the wife of an ambassador and mother to the thirty-fifth president of the United States and of two U.S. senators, Rose earned the title of "Political Matriarch." But perhaps the title she cherished most was "Grandmother." In fact she and her husband decided that even their children's spouses should refer to them as "Grandma and Grandpa." Jacqueline used her own pet name for Rose, "Belle Mère," a French endearment meaning a treasured mother-in-law.

Joan and Ted Kennedy with Rose at St. Ann's, West Palm Beach, Florida, 1977.

In her lifetime Rose was grandmother to twenty-eight grandchildren. As a hands-on leader of the family and role model, she was full of advice and old-fashioned expressions that often caused her grandchildren to giggle. "'On your toes' was a favorite saying that may have had more impact on her children than the younger generation," said Davidoff. Her close friend Mary Sanford once remarked that "Rose didn't have patience for things she thought were frivolous." Davidoff remembered Rose as a woman of action who did not tolerate laziness, even though her grandchildren were on vacation. There was church to attend, golf and tennis games, social outings, movies, biking across the island, and all sorts of water activities. But most importantly there was the family, and she was a big promoter of the interaction between her grandchildren.

Because she was a woman who packed a lot of action into one day, she adopted the habit of pinning notes to her dress when she was in the house to remind her of her children's appointments, social schedules, menus, charity duties, and other tasks that needed to be accomplished. As each assignment was completed, the corresponding note was ripped off and thrown in the wastepaper basket. Those who knew her well thought nothing of meeting Rose at the house with ten notes safety-pinned to her dress. "It was a bouquet of reminders," Davidoff remembered. "Some people use date books or attach notes to cork boards—Rose liked to keep her obligations and appointments pinned to her heart."

Rose became legendary for her note writing. When her son Jack was on the campaign trail she would slip him a note about what to wear at the podium. She sent notes to her daughters about the importance of always traveling with calling cards. No matter where in the world or what stage of life

Rose Kennedy votes for her favorite democrat in Palm Beach, February 2, 1976.

her children and grandchildren were experiencing, Rose's notes of encouragement and advice would find their way to boarding schools, summer camps, vacations, even on the eve of important events such as a wedding or a presidential election.

Rose Kennedy getting into her car on Worth Avenue. Frank Saunders, the Kennedys' chauffeur, and Davidoff were always joking. Here Davidoff is telling Saunders that the handbag goes very nicely with his shoes.

Rose Kennedy strolling down Worth Avenue. Behind her in the window are the large sunglasses that her daughter-in-law Jackie had made so popular. December 14, 1973.

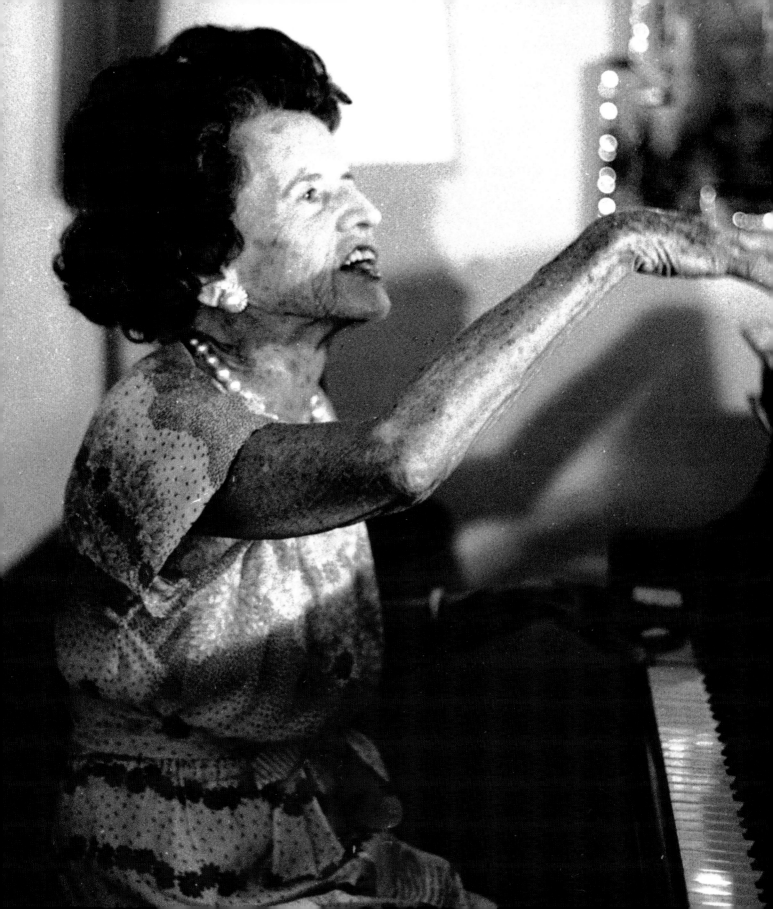

Rose leads a sing-along in her home,
March 5, 1979.

Rose and her daughter Pat at a benefit luncheon for Cystic Fibrosis at the Henry Flagler Museum, January 21, 1973.

NO SMOKING

The belles of the ball. Estée Lauder, Rose and Mary Sanford attend the
Red Cross Ball at the Breakers Hotel, Palm Beach, Florida, 1976.

Always by her side, Senator Edward Kennedy.

A note to her children, from *Times to Remember* by Rose Kennedy, dated June 19, 1958.

Dear Children:

This letter which I am sending to all of you may be of some help to you in the future.

When there is a clergyman present at a luncheon or at a dinner, the hostess asks him to say grace and no one is seated until after he has done so. The same thing applies at the end of a meal. . . .

When traveling abroad, bring calling cards with you. Send them to the embassy by courier or leave them yourself with the corner turned down and possibly the address of the hotel. You then will probably get a phone call for luncheon or tea. A lady is supposed to leave a card for every lady of the embassy. A man leaves them for every man, as well as for the ladies. For instance, last year when I was in London, I went to the embassy and left two cards: one for Mrs. Whitney and one for daughter Sara Roosevelt. If your father had been with me, he would have left three. However, you know your father.

Also, when you have gone to a luncheon at the home of an important person, it is well to leave a note of thanks immediately. For instance, when the Cardinal gave a luncheon for Grace Kelly, she wrote a note of thanks that very afternoon and it made a tremendous impression.

I am just giving you these few hints. Perhaps, if you follow them, you will be more of a success socially.

Much Love,
Grandma

CHAPTER TWO

CAMELOT BY THE SEA

President-elect John F. Kennedy greets
his supporters in West Palm Beach.

President John F. Kennedy, 1962.

AVIDOFF NEVER FORGOT THE CHANGE OF ATMOSPHERE IN PALM BEACH FOLLOWING THE PRESIDENTIAL ELECTION OF 1960. "The neighborhood boy was going to be the president of the United States," said Davidoff. "There was such pride among the residents. No matter how sophisticated people were, they were so excited."

Many Palm Beachers, regardless of whether they were Democrats or Republicans, sported JFK pins on their preppie Brooks Brothers shirts while strolling down Worth Avenue. And when the president-elect visited the island just several weeks after the election, thousands of people waited hours in the heat to greet their beloved son in the passing motorcade.

"Crowds lined the road from the airport all the way to Palm Beach, which is roughly three miles," said Davidoff. "They called his name, and he would reach out his hand to them and say hello. The women would swoon. He'd call some people by their name. The very fact that he recognized them was something they couldn't get over."

And it is no doubt why this tropical town was so familiar to the president. Palm Beach represented many wonderful childhood memories. The *Palm Beach Post* once wrote, "Jack Kennedy grew up with Florida sand in his shoes." It was at his parents' southern estate, where the young Kennedy ran freely down the beaches, sailed for hours on the Atlantic Ocean and enjoyed hamburgers with his brothers and sisters at the local drugstore, Green's Pharmacy. He was at home here.

As a presidential candidate, he chose Palm Beach as the place to plan his campaign, and later it would represent a relaxing haven from the oval office.

Davidoff always believed that Palm Beach was his perfect getaway. The residents knew him and let him rest. "It was hard always having the eyes of the world watching your every move. People here never gawked. They left him alone and at peace with his thoughts," Davidoff recalled.

THE PRESIDENT COMES TO TOWN

The president and his young family traveled to Palm Beach at least six times a year, sometimes spending lengthy periods of time relaxing, enjoying the company of other family members and, on certain occasions, conducting official White House business. Before the presidency, the Kennedys flew into Palm Beach Airport aboard their twin engine converted Convair called *The Caroline*. Now it was the presidential jet, *Air Force One*, that carried the young family to the Winter White House. And as always, Davidoff was there to greet the Kennedys with his camera.

"They didn't travel lightly," he recalled. "Out from the cargo hold appeared twenty different suitcases, presumably most of those belonging to Jackie. There were golf clubs, John-John's carriage, all sorts of sporting gear, fishing poles and of course the president's rocking chair. And they were just on vacation!"

At first the men at the airport in charge of loading were at a loss about how to get the large amounts of luggage over to the house. Eventually a large truck recruited from the Parks Department was found to shuttle the cargo to the Winter White House in just one trip.

President Kennedy, 1963. One of the few pictures of President Kennedy with a hat. Although popular at the time, Kennedy was not fond of wearing anything on his head.

President Kennedy and Jackie arriving at Palm Beach International Airport, 1962.

At the end of the holiday season the first family's cargo seemed to have multiplied. In the spring of 1963 a group of reporters watched as the luggage was loaded onboard *Air Force One*. The *Palm Beach Post* reported, "There were suitcases, sacks of oranges and grapefruits, a canvas-covered high-backed chair, two orthopedic mattresses and an electric device with a strap that looked like an exercise machine. It may have been the luggage of any health-conscious family except for an ominous, leather-covered box shut tight with two large locks. 'That,' said a White House aide, being properly evasive, 'is the family football.'"

Unloading the First Family's luggage from Air Force One, *Palm Beach Airport, November 1963. The president rarely traveled without his rocker.*

The Kennedy plane, The Caroline. *The Convair served as the campaign plane for the candidate until he took office.*

Christmas in Palm Beach. The town expresses a very public Merry Christmas to the first family, 1961.

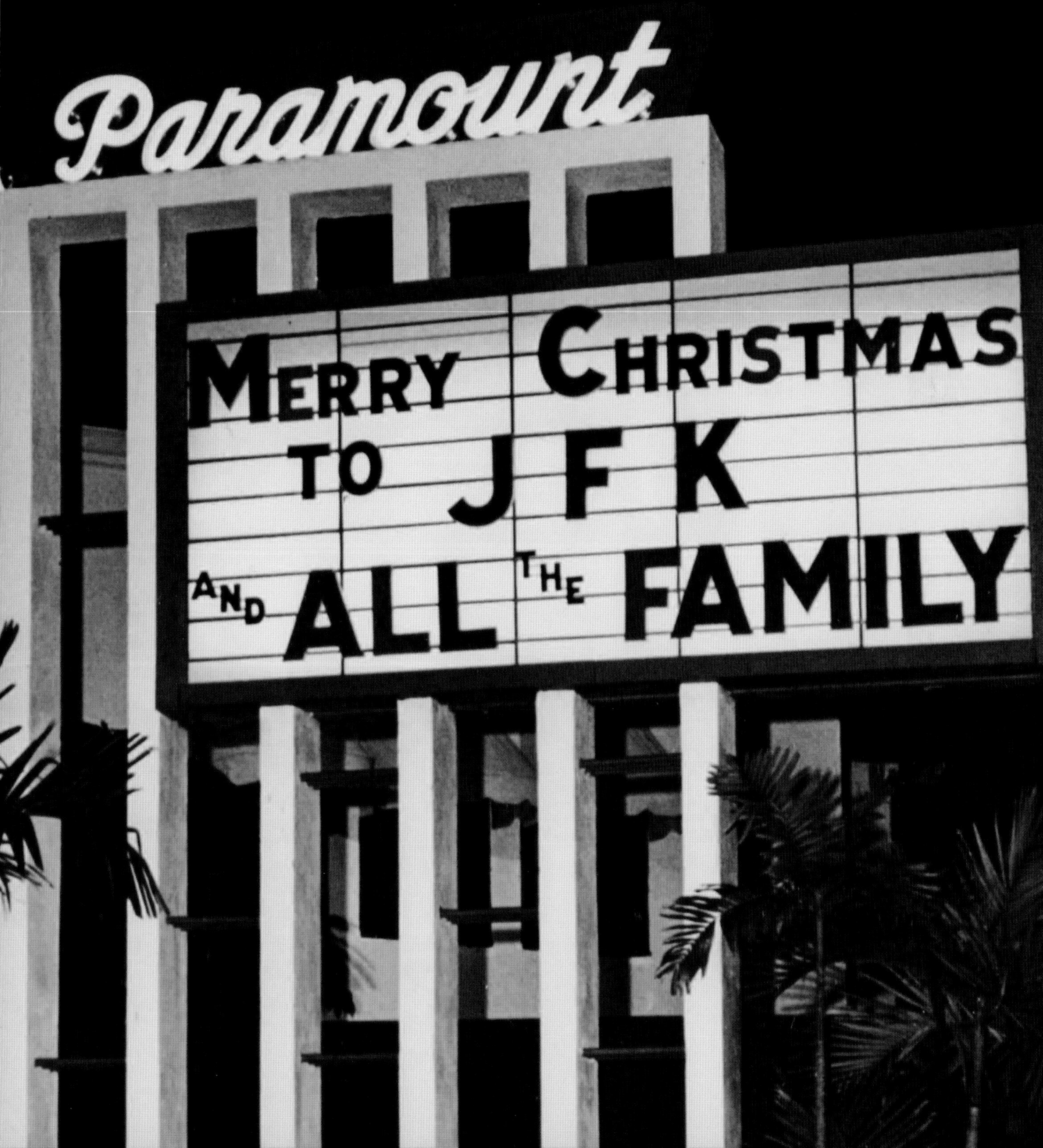
Paramount
MERRY CHRISTMAS
TO JFK
AND ALL THE FAMILY

THE PRINCESS OF PALM BEACH

No one on the island seemed more suited for the Palm Beach lifestyle than Jackie Kennedy. Her voracious taste for chic clothing was satisfied in many of the smart boutiques of Worth Avenue, and her love of stimulating conversation was fulfilled at the lavish parties attended by the likes of Truman Capote, Lilly Pulitzer, and Mrs. Lowell Guinness.

Jackie was no stranger to Palm Beach. She had visited the island quite frequently with her husband even before the presidency. In 1954 she spent many long weeks with him at the Kennedy home as he recuperated from one of his back operations. It was during those times that Jackie would start developing lasting friendships with different residents on the island. One such friend was Jayne Wrightsman, who hailed from an old Palm Beach family. In the years to come Jackie would spend many hours socializing and conversing about their shared interest in the decorative and fine arts. During the early sixties Wrightsman would play a resourceful role in Jackie's uncompromising vision for the restoration of the White House. After the president's death, it was at the Wrightsman's home, the elaborate estate named "Maison de l'Amitié," where Jackie would find comfort and rest from the tragedy.

Paul Bell (with National Airlines) helps Jackie and Caroline catch a plane at the Palm Beach Airport.

Jackie and Ari on Sailfish Club dock April, 1973.

The Honey Fitz

Florence Pritchett Smith, Earl E. T. Smith and Jackie Kennedy onboard the **Honey Fitz,** *1962.*

Jackie Kennedy with secret serviceman Clint Hill, 1963

The name of the Kennedy's estate during this time was changed to the Winter White House by the press. As it became a southern headquarters for the president, Jackie soon found herself sharing her quarters with a lot more people than just the extended family.

She once remarked, after convalescing in the home after the birth of John Jr., "It was so crowded that I could be in the bathroom, in the tub, and Pierre Salinger was holding a press conference in my bedroom."

Davidoff clearly understood Jackie's well-known passion for privacy. He was advised by one of the Secret Service agents to obtain her permission before a photograph was taken of the children and was told to never take a picture of her after she walked out from the beauty parlor. Photographers who didn't take note would find a Jackie under a huge scarf hiding her face and carefully concealed curlers. Ironically the head scarf would become one of her fashion signatures and even influence designers like Jean Patou and Karl Lagerfeld, who later included the kerchief look in a few of their collections.

Caroline holds her father's hand as they walk to an Easter egg hunt 1963.

Colonel C. Michael Paul's home.

KENNEDY WATCHING

When the Kennedys were in town, there was little to indicate the presidential presence, at least to the casual observer.

Before his election, John F. Kennedy would stay at his father's home, but that arrangement soon posed a problem considering the large entourage that traveled with the president. Because of the privacy and space required, the presidential family often stayed at the palatial home of a friend, Colonel C. Michael Paul, a retired army officer and financier. The magnificent residence was also more in line with the sophisticated tastes of the First Lady. The white regency home boasted eight bedrooms, a world-class art collection, a marble staircase and large floor-to-ceiling windows with a view of the sea, and in the backyard sprawled the large heated swimming pool, a prerequisite for the president's ailing back. But for all its opulence, the main advantage to the estate was the immense hedges that surrounded the property, offering complete seclusion.

Ready for the Florida sun, President Kennedy getting out of his convertible Lincoln.

With all of the exotic foliage that hid the home from the road, passersby weren't able to see the multitude of Secret Service men scattered about the grounds, including the men who patrolled the sea with submachine guns during the night. There was an X-ray machine that scanned all packages delivered to the house and a police officer right inside the gate checking the identity of anyone who ventured onto the property. Also hidden from view was an ornate fountain filled with lily pads. It was beside the tinkling fountain where Caroline and her little brother, John Jr., loved to play.

The First Family gets in the car and heads to Easter Sunday service, 1963.

President John F. Kennedy leaving
the Kennedy home.

John F. Kennedy Jr.

Tourists who vacationed on the island knew that a Kennedy sighting most likely took place on Worth Avenue, where the family shopped for clothes and holiday gifts, or perhaps at St. Edward's Catholic Church as the family exited mass on a Sunday morning. The only indication to churchgoers that a Kennedy was in attendance was a reserved pew for the family where Secret Service men positioned themselves on either side of the aisle. No one was aware of the "red phone" or the Army Signal Corps man seated in the back of the church with the secret codebook said to be in constant proximity to the president should he have to order a nuclear attack. After mass, the president would take time to pass a friendly word with old acquaintances or shake hands with a group of admirers who lined the front of the church.

It was the truly curious who would take more extreme measures to see the president, and their determination would often lead them out to sea, where the first family could often be seen enjoying an afternoon cruise aboard the presidential yacht, the *Honey Fitz*. One of Davidoff's favorite Kennedy sightings—or in this case "meeting"—took place when a catamaran carrying six area residents sped past the presidential yacht one beautiful spring afternoon in 1963. President Kennedy waved his arms to get the attention of the skipper. "When the sailboat pulled along the sailboat, Kennedy asked 'any chance of us hitching a ride,'" recalled Davidoff. "Well you can just imagine the look on the passengers' faces." The president jumped on board the catamaran with Undersecretary of the Navy Paul Fay and took control of the helm. At the end of the twenty-minute adventure, the president thanked the astonished skipper and returned to his yacht. "After the story got out about how the president hitch-hiked a ride on a stranger's boat," said Davidoff, "the water was suddenly teeming with hopeful sailors and dreams of a presidential encounter at sea."

The infamous "Red Phone" installed in the back of St. Edward's Catholic Church.

HERBERT HOOVER

JFK enters the home of H. Loy Anderson to meet former President Herbert Hoover.

Davidoff remembered Jack Kennedy as a man who could always find the humorous side of life, especially in front of a crowd.

"It just so happened one time that the president-elect and former president Herbert Hoover were in town at the same time," recalled Davidoff. "A prominent Palm Beach banker named H. Loy Anderson decided to hold a party in honor of Herbert Hoover and the christening of the Hoover Dike in Okeechobee, Florida, the very next day. Many people were invited, including John F. Kennedy and his father Joe.

Davidoff said that the ambassador urged his son to meet with the former president to collect a few words of wisdom. It could also prove to be a wonderful photo opportunity.

"There was this scene unfolding," said Davidoff. "The president-elect was reciting quietly in the corner what his father told him to say, and when he was ready he nodded for me to start taking pictures. He approached Hoover with his hand extended and said, 'Mr. President, I want you to know that I feel very proud to shake the hand of a past president, and I would like to know if you have any advice for me in terms of managing the country?'"

Davidoff said that Hoover nodded his head and said, "Nice to meet you."

"He kept shaking his head but still no answer to the question," recalled Davidoff. "Kennedy asked the question once more and again the same response. Then he turned to his father, trying to hold back a laugh and said, 'see those two hearing aids? He hasn't heard a goddamn thing I said!' so his father said, 'say it again very slowly and just let him read your lips.' Everyone had a little chuckle. It was embarrassing but very true to life."

*President-elect John F. Kennedy and
former President Herbert Hoover meet
for the first time. Hoover was in Florida
for the dedication of the Hoover Dike,
January 12, 1962.*

*JFK shares a private joke with his father
after he failed to notice that former
President Herbert Hoover is wearing
hearing aids.*

A SAD DAY

Davidoff remembered many long weekend visits by the president. "His parents were getting older, and he started to see his father slowing down," recalled Davidoff, "so the president wanted to spend as much time with them as possible."

In December 1961 Joe Kennedy took his son to the Palm Beach Airport to bid him farewell. As *Air Force One* headed back to the capital, a message was radioed to the pilot, and the plane was quickly turned back to Palm Beach. Joe Kennedy had suffered a stroke.

"When the president arrived with Jackie and his brother Robert, I was already at St. Mary's Hospital," said Davidoff. "They came out of the hospital about an hour later. Jackie was crying, visibly shaken. Robert and the president were also stunned and stood there deciding what to do. It was a sad day. Fortunately the ambassador pulled out of the stroke, but he would never fully recover. He remained partially paralyzed and confined to a wheelchair." This powerbroker and famous patriarch, a man who had served as an ambassador to Great Britain, was now facing the last years of his life. Davidoff remembered Joe Kennedy's love for his grandchildren, especially one afternoon as Ted's family was saying good-bye after a winter vacation in Florida. "Despite his condition, Kara and Ted Jr. ran up to jump in their grandfather's lap," recalled Davidoff, "The emotion he could no longer express verbally now glistened as tears in his eyes."

President John Kennedy and Jackie at St. Mary's Hospital, December 19, 1961.

Robert, Jackie and President Kennedy discuss the condition of the Ambassador after his stroke.

A grief-stricken Jackie gets in to the car with the president.

Ted Kennedy, Jr. and his sister with their beloved grandfather, December, 1965.

JOY RIDE

The first couple always felt relaxed and at ease when they arrived in Palm Beach. The president, who enjoyed dressing down in khaki slacks and penny loafers without socks, was known for his game of eluding his Secret Service men. He would often head behind the house pretending to go for a walk and take off toward his childhood haunt, Green's Pharmacy. According to Davidoff, Jackie, not one to be left out of the fun her husband was having with the Secret Service, decided to rent a convertible one day in order to meet her husband at the airport. She purposely failed to let anyone know of her plans. This, of course, broke all protocol when it came to security measures.

"She just wanted to be like your typical housewife picking up her husband after a business trip," said Davidoff. "As the president got off the plane Jackie ran down the tarmac screaming 'Jack, Jack, here I'll take you.' He got the biggest kick seeing Jackie and the kids in the car. He got in and then took off down the runway. The Secret Service was sent scrambling. It was a fun moment watching John driving his own car and leading the motorcade with all the sirens and lights."

Jackie surprises her husband at the airport with a rented convertible.

OFFICIAL BUSINESS

As Kennedy spent more time in Palm Beach, cabinet members, ambassadors and heads of state redirected their schedules to travel south for audience with the president. Joint Chiefs of Staff met in Palm Beach for defense talks and the president of Italy, Giovanni Gronchi sat amid the palms and the Kennedy pool to discuss the state of affairs in Europe. "With all of the dignitaries and country leaders flying into Palm Beach, they could have renamed the airport Dulles South," said Davidoff.

From greeting astronauts to ambassadors, the president was busy welcoming official visitors to the Sunshine State. "President Kennedy was always considerate of allowing time for pictures. But after a certain point," said Davidoff, "he would stop and just cut it off. He was gracious but impatient, always on the go. You had to do your job quickly. Otherwise, you would miss that 'Kodak' moment.'"

President John F. Kennedy with Italy's President Giovanni Gronchi and Heads of State, Palm Beach, Florida, 1962.

JFK with Mrs. John Glenn and family.

President Kennedy greeting the president of Italy Giovanni Gronchi at Palm Beach International Airport, 1962.

Members of the Bay of Pigs at the press room in the Palm Beach Towers. Left to right Alvaro Sanchez, Jose Perez San Roman, Dr. Manuel Artime, Press Secretary Pierre Salinger, Ernesto Oliva, State Department translator Enrique Ruiz–Williams, Roberto Perez San Roman.

President John F. Kennedy, Mrs. John Glenn and daughter Lynn at Palm Beach International Airport, July 1962.

President John F. Kennedy leaving the dock after sailing on the Honey Fitz, *1963.*

*President John F. Kennedy with
the president of Italy at Palm
Beach International Airport,
1962.*

*Vice President–elect Lyndon
B. Johnson, President John F.
Kennedy and House Speaker
Sam Rayburn pictured on the
Kennedy Estate's west patio.*

President Kennedy announces his cabinet outside the Kennedy estate. Left to right: Lyndon B. Johnson, President Kennedy, House Speaker Sam Rayburn and Senator Mike Mansfield, 1961.

JFK and good friend Stuart Symington.

THE *HONEY FITZ*

A favorite pastime of the Kennedys was taking friends aboard the presidential yacht. The 92-foot vessel built in 1933 was christened the *Lenore* and originally used by President Eisenhower. In 1961 President Kennedy renamed it the *Honey Fitz* after his beloved maternal grandfather, John F. Fitzgerald.

Most of the year the yacht was docked on the Potomac and periodically brought down by the navy for use by the first family in Palm Beach. The spacious yacht carried up to sixty people and proved to be a perfect vessel for entertaining guests in the Florida sun.

The Presidential yacht, the Honey Fitz.

"The yacht was actually more suited for the flat waters and fair weather of Palm Beach," recalled Davidoff. "It had plenty of open decks that allowed the family to enjoy a beautiful day on the intracoastal waterway."

Taking the yacht out on the open waters, however, proved to be a complicated procedure for the president's security team. In late 1960, right after the election, an assassination attempt on Kennedy in Palm Beach had the Secret Service on high alert.

"Many people don't know this, but this deranged man by the name of Richard Pavlick loaded his car up with enough dynamite to blow up a large building," said Davidoff. "His plan was to drive right up to the Kennedy home in Palm Beach and ram the president-elect's car and blow it up."

Pavlick waited patiently for Kennedy outside the home. But at the last minute the

John F. Kennedy leaves the presidential yacht, the Honey Fitz *to head back to Washington. Jackie gets off the yacht to say goodbye to her husband Palm Beach, 1963.*

future president's life was saved when the sight of Jackie walking out the door with her infant son in her arms quickly disarmed Pavlick, giving him a moment of conscience. He later admitted after his arrest that he did not wish to harm her or her children.

"So every time the family was in Palm Beach, the president was heavily protected," said Davidoff. "When the president went for a cruise, the *Honey Fitz* was escorted by a coastguard cutter, a high-speed chase boat, and a helicopter overhead. The only thing missing was a submarine!"

Due to the tight security, press photos were relegated to the pier, allowing Davidoff to document only the arrival and departure of the presidential yacht.

"One time, though, I did get an intimate shot of the president and first lady," chuckled Davidoff. "He was off to Washington again and just like a husband saying good-bye to his adoring wife before a business trip, he grabbed her up in his arms and gave her a long and loving embrace. I shot it, although I closed my eyes for a moment out of respect!"

Jack and Jackie embracing inside the yacht, 1963.

An Army helicopter arrives to pick up JFK and Jackie and take them to Miami where the president will address the Cuban population there. The helicopter would often land on a fairway of the Palm Beach Country Club, a short distance from the Kennedy home.

THE BAY OF PIGS

The Bay of Pigs invasion of Cuba took place April 17, 1961. The military maneuver supported by Kennedy failed miserably and marked the administration's first political setback.

"After the fiasco, Kennedy flew down to Palm Beach to meet with the survivors," remembered Davidoff. "He insisted they meet at the Kennedy home. He wanted some time alone with these men in a private place to tell him how bad he felt about the whole ordeal."

After a press conference with the survivors, the president and his wife boarded *Marine One*, which was waiting on a fairway at the Palm Beach Country Club. From there they flew to the Orange Bowl in Miami to address not only the Cuban population in South Florida but the people of the nation.

"It was a very somber occasion," recalled Davidoff, "I had never seen the president go through such strain. Actually I think it made him larger-than-life because it's not always taking credit for things that go right, but standing up for things that go wrong."

President Kennedy with the survivors of the Bay of Pigs on the patio of the Kennedy estate, April 1961.

President Kennedy and Jackie on the extreme right ready to board a helicopter that will take them to Miami to address the Cuban population there about the Bay of Pigs. Secret serviceman Clint Hill, walking in front of the helicopter, was in Dallas when Kennedy was shot.

The helicopter leaves the fairway at the Palm Beach Country Club. On left, Palm Beach Police Chief Homer Large.

FORE SCORE

The love of sport was an inherent trait in the Kennedy clan. Whether it was tennis, sailing, or some kind of contact sport, the Kennedys lived their vacations outdoors, immersed in athletic competition. Palm Beach boasted some of the best golf courses in the state, and the Kennedys took advantage of the privacy and challenge that the sport had to offer.

John F. Kennedy, his father Joe and his brother-in-law Peter Lawford get ready for a game of golf at the Palm Beach Country Club. The president would never be photographed with golf clubs; he felt it very un-presidential. 1961.

For President Kennedy, golf was the one activity that did not seem to aggravate his back ailments. Yet despite the fact he had played the game since his youth, it was widely known that he was far from a talented player.

"One time I got to the golf course to get a few newspaper photos of the president playing a round with his father, Peter Lawford, and a few of their friends," said Davidoff. "I was immediately handed a press release that said that I could take my pictures but that there will be no mention of the final scores."

One of Kennedy's perennial golf partners was a prominent Palm Beach businessman by the name of Chris Dunphy. "Dunphy was a hustler, so you always knew when those two got together on the golf course that there was a side bet going," said Davidoff. One time Davidoff was told by one of Kennedy's caddies about a heated and humorous banter between the two.

"The president was starting to lose pretty badly," said Davidoff, "so he started chiding Dunphy that if he didn't forgive a few of his strokes in the sand trap that he when he returned to Washington he was going to speak to the Internal Revenue Service about taking a closer look at Dunphy's tax returns."

JFK with his brothers-in-law Steven Smith and Peter Lawford, April 4, 1961.

Good friend Chris Dunphy and the president on their way to a dinner party.

THE GOLDEN EGG

Jackie and John Jr. on their way to Easter Mass at St. Edward's Church, Easter 1963. John holds tightly to his precious golden egg.

For devout Catholics like the Kennedys, a vacation in the sun did not mean a vacation from their faith. "When Rose's family stayed together," remembered Davidoff, "she made sure they prayed together!"

Every Sunday the family would head off to St. Edward's in Palm Beach, a Catholic church they had attended since 1933. "They had been attending St. Edward's so long that the family had their own pew," recalled Davidoff. The photographer especially enjoyed photographing the family at the church during a holiday, knowing it would be the perfect opportunity to gather the Kennedys all together for a group picture.

One of Davidoff's more famous photos captures the first family in 1963 on their way to Easter Mass. They had just attended an Easter egg hunt at the Wrightsman's home, and in one of the photos in the series John Jr. clutches a golden egg in his left hand.

"Jackie told me later how she adored that picture," recalled Davidoff, "because she is reminded of John's enthusiastic discovery of the golden egg and his reluctance to put his prize possession down all day. She said he fell asleep that night clutching the egg for dear life."

Many years later Davidoff read in the travel section of the *Palm Beach Post* that the picture she admired so much still sits framed on the dressing table of her childhood room at Hammersmith Farm in Rhode Island.

Jackie and Caroline get into to the special armored Lincoln, April 1963.

President Kennedy, Caroline, and a rambunctious John Jr.

Easter Sunday at the Kennedy home, April 1963.

The First Family back from Easter Sunday festivities, April 1963.

President John F. Kennedy with Caroline, Jackie, and John Jr., Easter 1963.

Jackie holds her energetic toddler John Jr., 1963

A giant chocolate Easter Bunny arrives for Caroline, April 1961.

THE LAST PHOTOGRAPH

On Friday, November 15, 1963, President Kennedy headed down for another long weekend, but this time it was strictly business.

Kennedy wanted to visit Cape Canaveral to watch the launch of a Polaris missile. Yet the reason for his trip was an announcement he was anxious to make in Palm Beach.

"He had a meeting Sunday morning with the state Democrats to tell them that during the re-election campaign next year he had planned to make Palm Beach campaign head-quarters," said Davidoff "He was definitely planning on spending more time here."

Late in the afternoon, as routine, Davidoff followed the motorcade to the airport. As Kennedy approached the plane, he shook hands and said good-bye to a few of the Florida statesmen that stood on the tarmac. "I raised my hand in a farewell wave, still clicking away," recalled Davidoff. "And with a big smile upon his face he returned the gesture and said 'see you in a couple of weeks.'"

Four days later, the president flew to Texas.

As President Kennedy leaves Palm Beach International Airport, Bob takes his last photograph of the president.

CHAPTER THREE

A TOWN IN MOURNING

Jackie and her sister Lee and husband
Stas Radziwill after the funeral in
Washington. Palm Beach, 1963.

WHEN PRESIDENT KENNEDY LEFT PALM BEACH IN NOVEMBER 1963, everyone expected him to return for the Christmas season. Plans were being made for his re-election, and Palm Beach was to play an important role as headquarters of his presidential campaign. But the winds of fate changed these hopeful plans. Davidoff was in his car when he first heard reports of the tragedy in Dallas. "The news on the radio overwhelmed me with grief, I could hardly drive. As the news of the JFK's assassination traveled throughout the country, a nation mourned, but nowhere was the news more of a shock than to the residents of Palm Beach."

The island had been home to the president since he was a small boy. As leader of the country, he selected Palm Beach as the location of the Winter White House. His love of the ocean was the main reason he chose the seaside location for relaxation as well as a place to conduct official business, which was often off the coast of Florida aboard the *Honey Fitz*.

As grief set in, residents who had known him for years struggled for words. Palm Beach Police Chief Homer O. Large, who had first met the president when he was fourteen years old, said, "What kind of statement can you make in a time like this? A friend you've known for a long time and was always so happy when he greeted you." Many area officials traveled to Washington for the president's funeral, including several Palm Beach County councilmen and the town's mayor. Florida Governor Farris Bryant declared November 25 a day of mourning and ordered all Florida government offices and schools closed.

In Palm Beach, the streets were empty. Shops, closed out of respect, displayed pictures of the president on their front windows. An elegant French restaurant was draped in black. Memorials were held in churches across Palm Beach County and special masses were said at the church where John F. Kennedy worshiped and had once served as an altar boy. Out of respect for the president, the Kennedy family pew at St. Edward's was kept vacant. Churchgoers left roses on the black-shrouded church, bench. A bereaved Monsignor O'Mahoney, pastor of St. Edward's church, told the *Palm Beach Post* that he recalled a

A grieving Jackie steps out of the Kennedy home in Palm Beach with her sister Lee Radziwill, 1963.

funny moment when he saw the president in Ireland that summer, "He introduced me to his friends as pastor of a humble church in the little village of Palm Beach. What a sense of humor that man had."

For the photographer who captured images of Kennedy during many of his joyous moments in Palm Beach, the tragedy was experienced in a very personal way. "It felt like I lost a family member," recalled Davidoff. "People here were always impressed at how the presidency never changed him. He had an electric personality and a great sense of humor. He wasn't in any situation where he didn't look at the humorous side." Several nights after the assassination, the photographer drove around the area and witnessed a town in mourning. In the windows of many Palm Beach homes glowed the flickering flame of a single candle. "It was," felt Davidoff, "as if the residents were waiting for their beloved son to return home."

THE HEALING YEARS

Rose once told Davidoff after the tragedies that befell her family in the sixties, "After you grieve you can decide either to go on or to join them." Her choice to go on and flourish served as an act of strength that was modeled by her children and grandchildren for years to come.

One of Davidoff's first photographs of the family after the assassination was of Jackie, dressed in mourning clothes in front of the Palm Beach estate. It was here on the island that she chose to start the healing process. "She would often fly down on the red eye from New York," recalled Davidoff. "Palm Beach afforded her the rest and privacy she sought after the tragedy."

The two senators, Edward and Robert, also made their way south to seek solace in the sun. A grieving Robert, who was having a particularly hard time with his brother's death, came to Palm Beach quite often in the winter months to look after his ailing father. Just two years before, Joe Kennedy had suffered a stroke in Palm Beach, which left him partially paralyzed and confined to a wheelchair. It was Robert who looked after the ambassador, and for a short time up until his death in 1968, Robert served as the head of the extended Kennedy family.

Rose also found comfort in Palm Beach. As she had always taken to walking the expansive stretch of beach behind her home as a comfort in times of crisis, she and her husband decided to make their way down to Palm Beach after the funeral. She recalled in her memoirs how the family headed south in late November 1963 to get away from the sadness and to celebrate "Christmas in the usual way—the big tree and all of the trimmings—and some of the grandchildren were able to be there. They all came for visits that winter and spring as often as they could to cheer up our lives."

Rose kept herself busy the first few months after her son's death by answering some of the thousands of condolence letters

The entranceway of the Kennedy home decorated for Christmas. Later the doors of the home were granted historic landmark status.

that poured into the Kennedy home. Those that she could not answer personally were taken over by her daughters. She also greeted well-wishers to her home, one of them being President Lyndon Johnson and his wife Lady Bird, who stopped by to pay their respects on their way to a Democratic fundraising dinner in Miami.

Davidoff too wanted to pay his respects, and to say something of comfort when he came by to take the family's pictures for the press. "When I got close enough to Jackie, I looked at her, and she said she knows, it was almost as if she was reading my mind," remembered Davidoff, "it was that way with the rest of the family too. I guess friends must know when you empathize with them."

Robert Kennedy,
January 20, 1965.

Senator Edward "Ted" Kennedy
at the doorway of the Palm Beach
estate, December 1964.

{ T h e   K e n n e d y   F a m i l y   A l b u m }

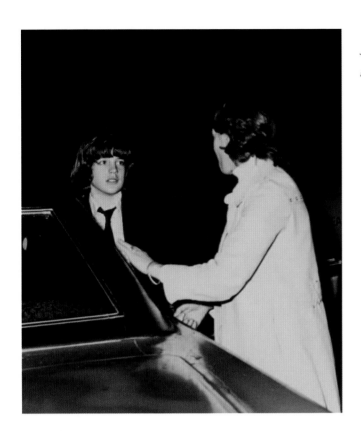

John F. Kennedy Jr. with his governess, March 3, 1973.

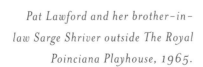

Pat Lawford and her brother-in-law Sarge Shriver outside The Royal Poinciana Playhouse, 1965.

Jackie and her children, John Jr. and Caroline, attend mass at St. Edward's Catholic church, Palm Beach, Florida, April 14, 1968.

Caroline, John Jr. and Jackie walk into church, April 14, 1968.

Umbrellas and an Easter basket.
Jackie, Caroline and John Jr.
take shelter from the rain.
April 14, 1968.

John Jr., April 1968.

John Jr. shielded from the rain as he heads to the plane.

Rose Kennedy with her grandson Robert Shriver.

A JOURNALIST IN THE MAKING

Although the years between 1963 and 1968 were marked with great loss and challenges for the Kennedys, Davidoff's photos show a family carrying on with their lives with great courage and grace. Laughter and love of tradition continued with gusto. Christmases were celebrated with the largest tree the family could find. After dinner Rose would lead

The Shriver children pose with Santa, played by the Kennedy chauffer, December 25, 1964.

group sing-alongs in the living room, teaching the grandchildren her favorite song, "My Wild Irish Rose." The Kennedy pastime of roughhousing and practical joking was already becoming apparent in this newest generation of Kennedys.

One of Davidoff's favorite photographs during this time shows the young Shriver children gathering around Rose's chauffeur, Frank Saunders, who is disguised as Santa Claus. Maria stands apart from her brothers, wearing a devilish grin as if she is ready to expose a secret. "Maria was trying to pull off Santa's beard," remembered Davidoff. "She kept saying, 'You're not Santa, you're Grandma's driver.' Frank quickly shot back with a curt whisper, 'If you don't be quiet, kid, I'll break your little arm.' Apparently it worked. She shut right up."

Maria was always impressing Davidoff, even when she was a little girl. One time when he was called out to take pictures of the Kennedys, he was greeted outside the estate by a reporter with the White House press corps who looked a bit flustered. The man was hanging around the house looking for stories about the family. Instead Maria decided to turn the tables on the situation by insisting on interviewing the reporter. "It was a picture that had to be taken," laughed Davidoff. "Just to think I documented Maria Shriver's first interview!"

Maria Shriver conducts her first interview outside the Kennedy home in Palm Beach.

THE PURPOSEFUL KENNEDY

Perhaps the Kennedy Davidoff knew the least was Robert Kennedy. Unlike his brothers Jack and Ted, Robert was not a regular visitor to Palm Beach. With ten children in tow, it wasn't easy to make the trip so often. But Davidoff speculated that it was Robert's lifelong work and concern for the poor that may have made it hard for him to enjoy the opulence of Palm Beach.

With his brother Jack gone, Robert took on a supporting role in the family, quite literally. Beyond continuing the mission of the late president, he uplifted his brother's grieving widow and became a surrogate father to her children. And he honored his mother with his frequent visits. But it was his loyalty to his father that started Robert coming to Palm Beach on a regular basis, along with his painful attempt to rehabilitate his father, who was left partially paralyzed from his stroke. Davidoff remembered how he would sometimes fly to Palm Beach first thing in the morning from Washington to check on his father and then fly back in time to be home for dinner with his family.

Senator Robert Kennedy arrives at Palm Beach after attending President Johnson's inauguration earlier in the day. When asked by reporters his reason for coming to Florida, his only comment was, "To see my father." January 20ᵗʰ, 1965.

Devoured by grief, Robert Kennedy's face showed signs of pain and the heavy burden of self-imposed responsibility. His visits to the Sunshine State during this

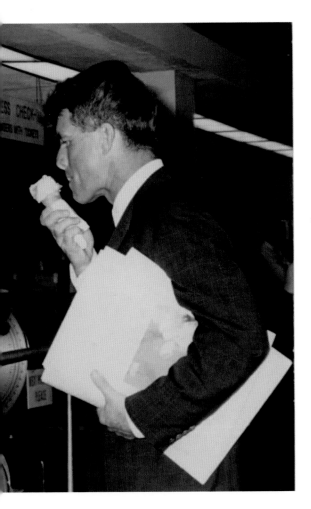

time were not attached with the pleasurable activities associated with vacation. They were trips of purpose. In January 1965 he flew down to Palm Beach to personally deliver the news to his father that Lyndon B. Johnson was re-elected, a bitter pill for the Kennedys because that was the election that was to be won by Jack. Also that same year, as keeper of the Kennedy legacy, the senator headed south to help raise money for The JFK Library at a fundraiser in Miami. The last time Davidoff saw Robert was with his wife, Ethel, as he was campaigning for president of the United States. "It was just four months before he was shot in Los Angeles," said Davidoff. "As a photographer I study faces, and it seemed like the mask of sadness had finally lifted from his face. He was now looking ahead with ideas and goals that might have changed a nation."

Robert Kennedy loved eating ice cream. No matter where he was, at the airport, at home, or on the campaign trail, Kennedy always completed the day with a big bowl of ice cream. Chocolate was his favorite flavor.

Robert Kennedy, January 14, 1964.

Robert and Ethel Kennedy at Palm Beach International Airport, February, 5, 1968.

Senator and Mrs. Robert Kennedy and former Secretary of the Treasury Douglas Dillon, February 1968.

Ethel and Robert Kennedy on their way back to Washington, February 5, 1968.

Robert Kennedy at a fundraiser for
the JFK Library held at the Diplomat
Hotel in Hollywood, Florida, 1965.

Robert Kennedy with Carol
Courshon at the Diplomat Hotel.

Robert Kennedy with Arthur Courshon.

115

THE SENATOR

Senator Ted Kennedy survived a plane crash in 1964. After many months of rehabilitation for a broken back, the senator finally walks without a cane, April 4, 1965.

A familiar smiling face in many of Davidoff's pictures was Edward Kennedy. The senator would frequently come down to Palm Beach with his family, and when his plane landed at the Palm Beach airport, he was often greeted by Davidoff. Kennedy would remark many times, "Oh, it's Bob Davidoff, Palm Beach's official greeter!" Over the years the photographer and the senator developed a light and joking relationship filled with laughs and comical remarks.

Just like his brother the president, Teddy enjoyed the ocean. One year the senator brought down the Kennedy family yacht, the *Marlin*, from Hyannis Port to entertain congressman-elect John Tunney and his family. On a beautiful New Year's day the group sailed from Palm Beach down the Intracoastal and into the Atlantic Ocean for a day cruise. "The senator took the helm of the large boat like a true captain," remembered Davidoff, who snapped pictures from the pier.

After his father suffered his stroke, Teddy stood by his mother, escorting her to Sunday mass with his wife, Joan, and to many of the Palm Beach events of the social season, including the prestigious Red Cross Ball.

Despite family tragedies over the years, Palm Beach was always a special memory for Senator Kennedy. It was the place of happy times with his brothers around the pool as they all caught up on family news as well as the spot of joyous Christmases and relaxing Easter vacations. It was also where he started one of his favorite pastimes. Ted Kennedy once told the writer Paul Reid of the *Palm Beach Post* how Jackie indirectly got him interested in painting when she encouraged her husband Jack to paint as a way to get his mind off the pain after his back surgery. In the typical Kennedy competitive fashion, his brother challenged him to take up the paintbrush.

"He decided we should both paint the same scene," said Ted, "and then in the evening have our family and friends critique them—without telling who painted which one. He had a real talent and bested me in the contest, but he started me on a lifelong hobby."

Davidoff was a recipient of that lifelong hobby, when Senator Kennedy presented him with a watercolor of a sailboat he painted in 1998. "The painting was very professional," said Davidoff. "It's a talent that most people don't even know about. Who knows, maybe when he sometimes gets weary from the stresses in Washington, he may have wished he'd become an artist!"

Ted Kennedy Christmas shopping on Worth Avenue, Palm Beach, Florida, December 1968.

Joan and Ted Kennedy

James J. Kilpatrick (left) and Senator Kennedy (right) at NACDS meeting.

Ted and Joan leave St. Edward's Church, December 25, 1964.

119

Ted's children, Kara and Ted Jr., playing a game on the tarmac waiting for their father's plane to arrive.

Ted Kennedy Jr. and Kara Kennedy with their friends.

Ted Kennedy's children, December 1969.

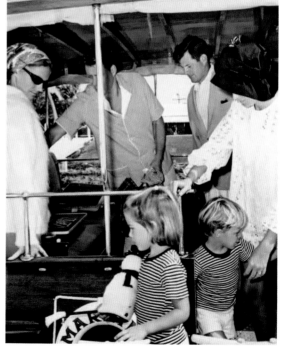

Congressman-elect John Tunney, son of former heavyweight champion Gene Tunney, with Senator Ted Kennedy and Ted Jr., New Year's Day, 1965.

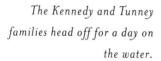

The Kennedy and Tunney families head off for a day on the water.

Congressman–elect John Tunney and Senator Ted Kennedy,
January 1, 1965.

Ted Kennedy at the helm of the Kennedy yacht, The Marlin, *Palm Beach, 1965.*

Ted Jr. and sister Kara on the stern of The Marlin. *Ted and Joan entertain their guests Congressman-elect John Tunney and his family, on Lake Worth, 1965.*

Ted Kennedy, Ted Jr. and Joan Kennedy, December 28, 1973.

Sometimes when the Kennedy family left the island of Palm Beach to go to church at St. Ann's Catholic Church in West Palm Beach they would stop traffic. Here Rose, Joan, and Ted are besieged by admirers seeking handshakes and autographs. Traffic came to a halt to watch the scene unfold, February 13, 1967.

CHAPTER FOUR

THE ONASSIS YEARS

S A WIDOW JACKIE STILL MADE FREQUENT TRIPS TO PALM BEACH TO VISIT DEAR FRIENDS, SHOP ON WORTH AVENUE AND BRING HER CHILDREN DOWN FROM HER HOME IN NEW YORK CITY TO SPEND VACATIONS AND HOLIDAYS WITH THEIR GRANDPARENTS. But in the spring of 1968 she would travel to the island with more than just Caroline and John. It was during a Kennedy Easter celebration that Jackie decided to introduce members of the Kennedy family to her old friend and future husband, Greek shipping magnate Aristotle Onassis.

"At that time Jackie and Ari didn't want the public to know they were an item, so when they flew into Palm Beach aboard one of Onassis's Olympic Airways jets, they made sure there wouldn't be any pictures of them together," recalled Davidoff.

Tipped off to their arrival, Davidoff positioned his car on the tarmac and waited for their plane. "The jet landed, and Jackie got right off with the two children in tow. She happily smiled for the camera and then drove off in a limousine," explained Davidoff. "I knew Onassis was still on the plane and was just waiting for me to disappear so he could disembark. I had brought my son Ken, and we were prepared to wait for hours if necessary."

Finally a stewardess emerged from the plane and informed Davidoff that the plane was empty. When Davidoff inquired about the whereabouts

Ari Onassis as he arrives in Palm Beach, March 5, 1973.

Prior to his romance with Jackie, Onassis often visited Palm Beach with Maria Callas.

of Onassis, she assured him that he was never aboard the plane. "I told her I'll just wait. I have nothing else to do," recalled Davidoff. Minutes later Onassis appeared and walked toward the car to have a chat with the photographer. Ken Davidoff, with a camera in hand, recorded the moment. "Onassis said to me, 'You know, you may think I am Aristotle Onassis, we look very much alike, and people are always confusing us. Actually I am his cousin.'" Davidoff countered by saying, "That's funny, because I photographed you not too long ago in Palm Beach with Maria Callas, and you are a dead ringer for him."

During this trip, Jackie and Ari retreated to the Wrightsmans' home, making an effort to stay clear of the press. "Our pictures of that night," said Davidoff, "were the only proof they had been together in Palm Beach."

Ari Onassis regularly flew to Palm Beach aboard one of his private planes.

Ari confronts Bob as Ken Davidoff, Bob's son, captures the moment with his camera.

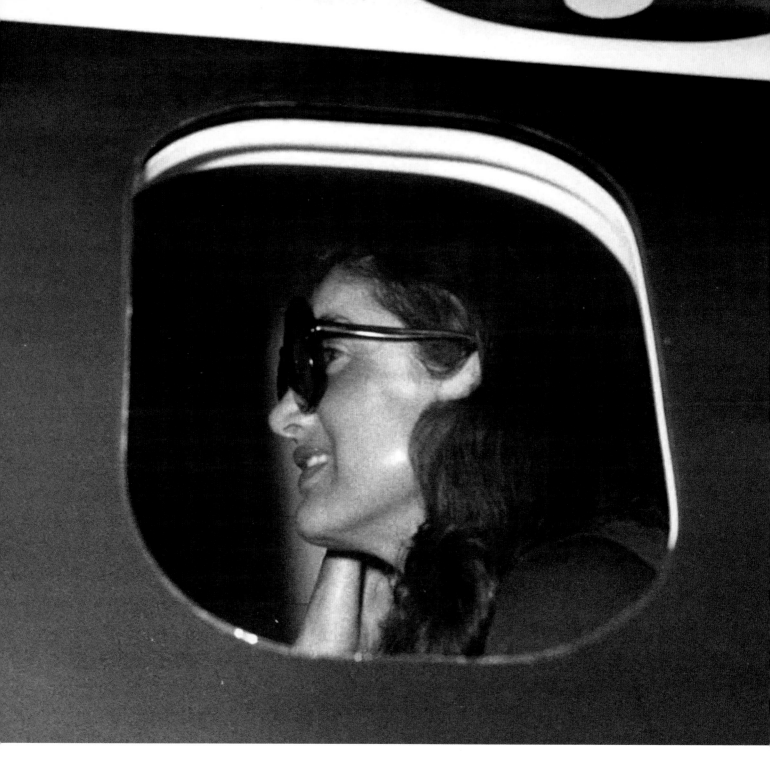

Jackie arrives from Greece for a restful vacation in Palm Beach, March 1973.

Jackie and Ari Onassis.

Ari Onassis and Winston Churchill, April 1961.

Jackie Onassis at Palm Beach International Airport.

Bob walking with Jackie as they talk about their children, March 1973. Bob's diminutive height was an advantage to him as a photographer. Bob said that "competing against a group of photographers, I could just duck on through the crowd without ever being noticed."

JACKIE O.

Davidoff recalled the two Jackies that came to visit Palm Beach over the years. "Jackie Kennedy was reserved, shy and introspective," said Davidoff. "She was regal with a certain innocence about her."

And then there was Jackie Onassis. Davidoff describes a woman with a newfound confidence and an air of independence both socially and financially. "If Jackie was once the princess of Palm Beach, she was now the Queen of Worth Avenue," said Davidoff.

"She loved to entertain, she loved to socialize, and she loved to shop" remembered Davidoff. "With an unlimited budget she could go into a store and buy ten thousand dollars worth of clothing in twenty minutes. She was a speed shopper. She knew exactly what she liked, and when she loved an item of clothing, she would buy one in every color. She didn't bother with prices or trying on the clothes, she would just point and charge. It was fascinating to watch."

Married to one of the world's richest men, Jackie now enjoyed enormous wealth and, most importantly, the protection she desperately sought after the assassination of her husband and most recently her brother-in-law Robert Kennedy. "She found a refuge in which to hide herself and her children" said Davidoff. "By taking them off to Europe, away from the public eye, she felt they were safe. When they were aboard *The Christina*,

Jackie Onassis in the head scarf and large sunglasses she made so fashionable.

there were a number of armed guardsmen and police dogs to protect the children."

During the Onassis years, "Jackie watching" was at the height of its popularity. It was at this time that Jackie started wearing the large sunglasses that quickly became one of her fashion signatures. Many fashion experts assumed it was to hide her identity, but it was revealed to her friend André Previn over lunch one day that the large dark glasses actually provided a certain amusement for her. The great composer and conductor asked if it bothered her that people were always staring at her. She replied, "That's why I always wear my dark glasses. It may be that they're looking at me, but none of them can tell which ones I'm looking back at. This way I can have fun with it!"

Jackie Onassis attending church services with her niece Maria Shriver.

Jackie Onassis.

Jackie and Charles Wrightsman,
April 15, 1968.

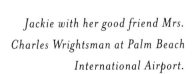

Jackie with her good friend Mrs.
Charles Wrightsman at Palm Beach
International Airport.

Jackie Onassis,
March 11, 1973.

John Jr. and Jackie, April 6, 1973.

Onassis's yacht "The Christina"
anchored off the coast of Palm Beach.

THE GREAT
CHRISTINA

Palm Beach was certainly the place of superlatives. The largest homes, the greatest private collections of artwork, and the most impressive yachts were in abundance on the island of wealth and fortune. Yet when the great vessel, *The Christina,* dropped anchor for the first time off the coast of Palm Beach, the floating palace redefined a new category in luxury and splendor.

"*The Christina* was so large that it was impossible to moor her next to the other yachts in the harbor," said Davidoff, "so Onassis had to anchor her offshore and take a private launch to the island."

Originally built in 1943 as a Canadian convoy escort, Onassis purchased the yacht in 1954. After he poured more than $4 million into refitting the vessel into a private luxury yacht, *The Christina* quickly became the most advanced pleasure craft afloat. "If Onassis liked showing off his wealth, it was certainly evident with the extravagance of *The Christina,*" said Davidoff. "I had seen opulence before, with the yachts of Palm Beach residents like the Kimberleys and the Benson Fords, but this was in a different league. *The Christina* was plain decadent."

"*The Christina* was closely compared to a ship in size, boasting 325 feet in length. There were 42 telephones, a doctor's office, a beauty salon, movie theater and 18 staterooms. And then there were the features that made this particular yacht legendary: such as the gold-plated bathroom fixtures, onyx and lapis lazuli fireplaces, a helicopter pad, and a handrail made of solid ivory, along with bar stools upholstered with the scrotums of whales, a fact that Onassis delighted in telling his guests.

"I happened to like the inlaid floor of the swimming pool, which was copied directly from the Palace of Knossos in Crete. With just a push of a button the bottom would rise to become a dance floor" said Davidoff. "The entire yacht lent itself to legendary entertaining."

"For years the guest list aboard *The Christina* was certainly the who's who of Hollywood stars, famous artists and writers, and international dignitaries," recalled Davidoff. "Winston Churchill came aboard many times and would use the fantail of the yacht as his floating art studio."

Instead of holding court at the Kennedy estate as she did in the early sixties, Jackie now entertained in style aboard the lavish mega-yacht. She invited her famous friends and family for weekend jaunts to the islands.

"It suited Jackie just fine," said Davidoff. "Now she didn't have to be under the footsteps of her mother-in-law, Rose. Even though the Kennedy estate was large, it was not large enough for two huge personalities. Jackie could go to the estate, make her obligatory visits with the children, and then literally cruise!"

In her day "The Christina" was one of the largest private yachts in the world.

The infamous mosaic
swimming pool aboard
"The Christina."
At night the floor of the
swimming pool was raised
and converted into a dance
floor.

Palm Beach Dock master Rod
Lavell presents a nautical
piece of art that he made for
Ari Onassis at the Sailfish
Club, April 1973.

Jackie with her sister Lee Radziwill.

Jackie, Maria Shriver, Caroline and John Jr. at the Sailfish
Club docks on their way to board The Christina.

Christina Onassis at Palm Beach International Airport, April 2, 1973.

John Jr.

A BOAT OF HIS OWN

Aristotle Onassis was determined to win the affection of his stepchildren, John Jr. and Caroline. In typical tycoon fashion he began showering them with expensive gifts: Shetland ponies, a jukebox and a mini-jeep to ride around the island of Skorpios were just some of the presents that represented his generosity.

As a shipping magnate and collector of commercial and luxury vessels, it seemed appropriate that Onassis would share his maritime interests with his stepson. "One day I get a call from the Dock Master at the Sailfish Club in Palm Beach," recalled Davidoff. "He said, 'you have got to see what Mr. Onassis bought for John Kennedy before I deliver it to him.'"

The gift was a brand-new, twenty-foot SeaCraft, completely outfitted for deep-sea fishing. "It was a great present for a twelve-year-old. The problem was John was hardly old enough to operate it himself," said Davidoff.

The boat was issued a captain and before long the SeaCraft went out to sea, taking John and his cousin Tony Radziwill on weekly fishing excursions. "They were typical kids. After an hour of fishing they would start to tease each other," remembered Davidoff. "The antics would include chasing each other around the deck until someone ended up in the water!"

John Jr. and his cousin Anthony Radziwill off on a fishing excursion, Palm Beach 1973.

CHAPTER FIVE

SUN, SAIL AND SKI

Bob Davidoff, Ted Kennedy and Joe Kennedy after a day of sailing off the coast of Hyannis Port, 1975.

T WAS IN THE MID-SEVENTIES THAT DAVIDOFF BEGAN TO LEAVE THE CONFINES OF PALM BEACH AND TRAVEL TO OTHER VACATION DESTINA- TIONS WITH THE KENNEDY FAMILY. Still working for United Press Interna- tional, the photographer first visited the Kennedy's summer home in Hyannis Port, Massachusetts, in early September 1975. Known as the "Kennedy Compound" because the grounds consists, of not one but several homes for the family, the property has served as a seasonal getaway for the Kennedys ever since Joe and Rose purchased the estate in 1929.

Ethel Kennedy with her daughters and nieces sailing off Hyannis Port, Massachusetts, 1975.

For years the main house and lawns overflowed with happy chaos as Rose's children and eventually grandchildren enjoyed summers together playing touch football, competing in sailboat races, and relishing in the joys of a family reunion. At grandma's house, as the compound was affectionately thought of, Rose kept her grandchil- dren happy by spoiling them with all their favorite foods. Creamed chick- en, Boston cream pie, and apple jelly were served in great abundance along with other Kennedy favorites like clam chowder, roasted chicken, and acorn squash.

"The Hyannis Port home really served as a backdrop for Ken- nedy family gatherings over the years," said Davidoff. "Memorable events were celebrated here, like birthdays and christenings, gradu- ations and homecomings. In fact several of the grandchildren chose

Hyannis Port as the location for their wedding receptions." Many of these milestones were evidenced by framed photographs and mementoes scattered throughout the large white gabled house by the sea. One photograph, prominently displayed in the living room, was taken on election night and shows the whole family—Rose, Joe, wives, husbands, brothers, sisters, and an exuberant young Jack who had just won the presidency. When Davidoff came to Hyannis Port that summer, he noticed the absence of photos in Jackie's home. She told Davidoff she felt it was still too early to look at pictures of her deceased husband. "The home was so special to her, because it contained so many memories," recalled Davidoff. "She had kept everything the same from the time she shared the cottage with the president. Even his jacket was still hanging on the back of the chair."

Most of the grandchildren were in attendance the summer Davidoff came to visit with his camera. "I was right there before all the cousins had to get back to school, so there was this end-of-the-summer feeling," recalled Davidoff. "They were playing touch football

Sargent Shriver and Eunice in Hyannis Port, 1975.

with a passion, swimming with a passion and sailing. . . . Well let's just say some family members excelled in the sport and some just plain capsized." One of Davidoff's favorite photo series shows a comical scene unfolding in the bay of Cape Cod. An embarrassed John Kennedy Jr. had capsized his boat along with his sailing partner and cousin Sidney Lawford. Before long a mop-topped gaggle of Kennedy cousins arrive on the scene in a speed-boat driven by William Kennedy Smith and nearly hit the overturned sailboat, already sinking fast. With everyone in good humor, the group completed the rescue and promptly sped away.

Six months later the fun-loving clan gathered together in Sun Valley, Idaho, for a week of skiing. Again Davidoff remembered plenty of joking and heated competition as the family took to the slopes of Bald Mountain. The most memorable picture of that trip shows the family patriarch, Ted Kennedy, waving from a sleigh filled with Jackie, Joan, and a host of laughing children.

In the spring of 1976, Jackie and John Jr. headed for the beaches of Jamaica. They were invited to the island by bandleader Peter Duchin and his wife, Cheray, who hosted the two at their home in Montego Bay. Davidoff clicked away as the fifteen-year-old John Kennedy conquered the beach with his tanned good looks and emerging sex appeal. "There wasn't a girl within six miles of that beach who wasn't flirting with John," laughed Davidoff. "You can see from the pictures that he was already in control of his charm and that the attention he received was something he didn't mind in the least!"

John Kennedy received four stitches in his head at an area hospital after the dingy he and cousin Vickie Lawford were crewing capsized in the late summer of 1975. John and Vickie were rescued by cousin William Smith.

Senator Edward Kennedy, his wife, Joan, Jackie Onassis and the Kennedy cousins take a sleigh ride to the Trail Creek Cabin, a restaurant located in a mountainside home that once belonged to writer Ernest Hemingway. Sun Valley, Idaho, January 1976.

William Kennedy Smith and a team of cousins to the rescue.

Victoria Lawford ducks as her brother Chris throws Caroline Kennedy off the dock in Hyannis Port.

Victoria Lawford,
Hyannis Port.

*Chris and Victoria
Lawford.*

*Bobby Shriver in Hyannis
Port, September 1975.*

*Edward Kennedy drives his nephews
back to the Kennedy Compound after
a day out in the water, Hyannis Port,
September 1975.*

John Jr. and Jackie Onassis at Caroline's high school graduation in Concord, Massachusetts, May 1975.

Maria Shriver in Hyannis Port, August 1975.

The Shriver Family pose for the camera at their home in Hyannis Port, August 1975.

*The young John Kennedy Jr.
and Jackie Onassis in
Hyannis Port, 1975.*

John Kennedy Jr. maneuvering
his bicycle, Hyannis Port,
September, 1975.

John Kennedy Jr.
accompanies his mother to
Jamaica for a vacation with
their friends the Duchins,
1976.

Jackie arriving in Jamaica,
West Indies, March 1976.

*Jackie Onassis and Cheray
Duchin, the wife of Peter Duchin,
in Jamaica, March 1976.*

John Kennedy Jr. goes for a swim off the beaches of Jamaica.

CHAPTER SIX

THE BEACH HOUSE

O THE WORLD THE HOME WAS KNOWN AS THE WINTER WHITE HOUSE, THE SETTING FOR CAMELOT BY THE SEA. IT WAS HERE BUT FOR ONE BRIEF SHINING MOMENT IN THE EARLY SIXTIES WHERE THE FIRST FAMILY CAME TO VACATION AND REST FROM THE STRESS AND STRAIN OF WASHINGTON AND THE PRESSURES OF PRESIDENTIAL LIFE. Since 1933, when Joe Kennedy purchased the home from department store magnate Rodman Wanamaker, the estate not only became a meeting place for the entire Kennedy family but also served as a historical backdrop as John F. Kennedy made some of the most crucial decisions during his presidency while staying at the seaside retreat. On the lawn facing the ocean, JFK spent many pensive hours working on his Pulitzer Prize-winning book, *Profiles in Courage* while recuperating from back surgery. He would later plan his presidential campaign on the terrace, write his inaugural speech by the pool, and announce his cabinet on the south patio of the estate. The home played host to high-ranking dignitaries and heads of state, and became a gathering place for famous astronauts, noted journalists and celebrities. And it was the venue of important and private meetings concerning the Bay of Pigs and the Cuban Missile Crisis. Yet despite the home's historical significance, to much of the Kennedy clan, the unassuming home at 1095 N. Ocean Boulevard was always lovingly referred to as the Beach House.

La Guerida, as its first owners called it, was not nearly as lavish as many of the other homes in Palm Beach. "There was no air, no heat, and sometimes when you walked on the floor you could feel the crunch of sand under your shoes," recalled Davidoff.

Leo Racine, one of the family's longtime aides in New York, managed the home after the ambassador died. He was responsible for getting the estate ready for the season. "After the home was closed during a long hot summer, I had to make the house livable," recalls Racine. The job was an arduous one, as mold and mildew crept through a roof that was often in need of repair. Windows and doors were left open for nearly a week to freshen up the enclosed rooms. "The curtains were bedraggled; the lack of air conditioner was the least of it."

Aerial view of the Kennedy estate in Palm Beach.

The lived-in atmosphere of the home is what appealed to the Shrivers. To them the estate was never viewed as a shrine. Here at the Beach House they gathered as a family, a time of reunion for most of them, who lived in different states. "I was over many times and the children were rowdy, running around, having fun. Sarge would be on the sofa with his feet up, watching a football game and drinking a beer," remembered Davidoff. "I would just go into the kitchen, and the cook would make me a sandwich. Everyone was very relaxed there."

Davidoff watched over the years as the young Kennedy cousins he met in the fifties and early sixties were coming down with kids of their own. A few of his photographs during the late seventies and early eighties reveal a proud Rose showing off her first great-grandchild and spending time socializing with her older grandchildren. She remained active in their lives despite her advancing years as she continued to take them to society parties, charity events and, of course, to church.

Because the extended Kennedy clan was becoming so large, each family member needed to reserve the home for their annual vacations in advance. Racine, acting as a concierge, would usually find himself booking the Shrivers for Christmas, Senator Edward Kennedy and his family around Presidents' Day, and Ethel and her brood sometime around Easter.

In April 1984 Rose suffered a stroke in the Palm Beach house. She was not aware that a few days later her grandson David died of a drug overdose at a nearby hotel. Davidoff was asked by UPI to cover the story. "It was very hard to see the family in so much pain," recalled Davidoff. "I was there during so many of their great moments, and now to be a witness to a dark moment was very sad to me."

It was just several months earlier when Senator Edward Kennedy had asked Davidoff to come to St. Edward's, the Catholic church where the Kennedys had worshipped for years, and take pictures of the family. Davidoff remembered an ailing Rose in a wheelchair, holding his hand and introducing him to Caroline Kennedy's fiancé, Ed Schlossberg. His last memory of Rose was when the Kennedy matriarch leaned over and whispered to her son Teddy, "Do you know how many years Mr. Davidoff has been our friend and taken our pictures?" "Here, after 25 years, she still called me Mr. Davidoff," remembered the photographer. "I liked that."

Grandma Rose and Caroline at a private party in Palm Beach. Rose told Bob, "If Caroline's mother knew she was wearing those cut-offs, she wouldn't be very happy!" March 1975.

Caroline greets the hostess of the party,
Mrs. Fanjul, March 1975.

Caroline with friend
and cousin Maria
Shriver as they head
into the water for a
swim, March 1975.

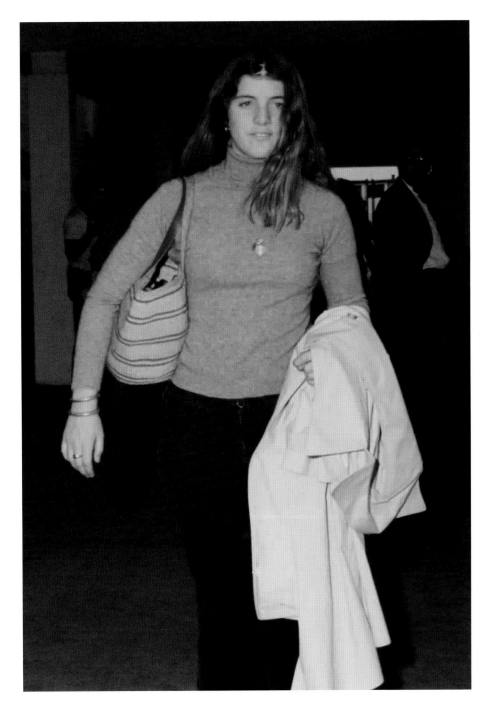

Caroline Kennedy at the West Palm Beach Airport, March 1975.

Caroline spends a day with her cousins at the beach behind her grandparents'
home in Palm Beach, 1975.

When Senator George McGovern arrived at Palm Beach International Airport, rumors started that Ethel Kennedy, the widow of Senator Robert Kennedy was there to endorse his bid for presidency. Later it was revealed that it was just two old friends meeting and sharing old times. March 9, 1972.

Giddy girls Ethel Kennedy and Maria Shriver head into the town of Palm Beach, 1973.

Senator Edward Kennedy and Ted Jr. getting ready for a bicycle ride
around the island of Palm Beach, December 23, 1973.

Sarge Shriver and his son Anthony

*Caroline Kennedy at the edge
of her teenage years, 1975.*

Rose hosts a benefit in her home for Retarded Children Charity, March 5, 1979.

Caroline and her fiancé Edwin Schlossberg on Christmas day, 1983.

Joan Kennedy and Bob Davidoff outside St. Edward's Church, April 1981.

Rose holds her first great-grandchild, Megan Townsend, with Megan's
parents, David and Kathleen (Kennedy) Townsend, 1978.

(left to right) Bobby Shriver, Ted Kennedy, Rose Kennedy, Eunice Shriver, Joan Kennedy, Patrick Kennedy, Timothy Shriver and Sarge Shriver standing outside St. Edward's Church, April 1981.

One of Bob's last pictures of Rose. Here she stands beside her son Senator Edward Kennedy.

CHAPTER SEVEN

FUTURE GENERATIONS

T HE KENNEDY ERA IN PALM BEACH ENDED IN 1993 WHEN, WITH HEAVY HEARTS, THE FAMILY PUT THE ESTATE UP FOR SALE. "I think it was a combination of Rose leaving Palm Beach because of her declining health and also the grandchildren were growing up and tending to their own families, that the house lost some of its allure," said Davidoff.

The last decade in Palm Beach were tough years for the Kennedys' once-unsullied image. The David Kennedy overdose and, although he was eventually acquitted, the William Kennedy Smith rape charge were additional marks against the Kennedys' reputation. Predicting that the trial was going to be a media circus, Davidoff was relieved that he no longer worked for UPI. He preferred to watch the coverage from a distance and met with a few Kennedys who were visiting the island at the time, knowing it would be the last time he would be seeing them on a regular basis.

The extended Shriver family for their last visit at the Kennedy estate.

The home with a history went on the market for $7.6 million, and because of the appeal of buying a piece of Camelot, the sale drew the interest of many wealthy, famous potential buyers, including singer Jimmy Buffett and his wife. But due to the deteriorated condition of the estate, many considered it a teardown, and so the house sat on the market for almost two years.

Davidoff had always wanted his wife, Babe, to see the place where he photographed all the wonderful Kennedy memories, and so one day he took her for a visit. What she found was a house that was gently worn and lovingly lived in. It was a home that revealed the personalities who lived there, especially that of matriarch Rose, whose bedroom walls were filled with pictures of the family, drawings from grandchildren, even a note to Santa that her youngest son Teddy wrote when he was seven years old.

Leo Racine often took potential buyers for a tour of the home, and it was perhaps his love for the property and the family he had worked for since 1948 that encouraged John K. Castle and his wife Marianne to buy the Kennedy estate. For almost five million dollars, the Castles purchased the house, and a whole lot of history, including the beds of Joe, Jack, Robert and Teddy, the president's mahogany massage table, and the eighteen-foot-long dining room table where the Kennedy clan gathered for sixty years. They even kept

Maria and Eunice Shriver take a final picture outside the Kennedy estate.

Leo—after all no one knew the estate and all of its quirks and crannies better than the loyal and longtime Kennedy aide.

Years after the sale of their beloved Beach House, a few members of the Kennedy family still make trips to visit the island. One of Leo's favorite stories is about the time a young man rang the doorbell and asked for a tour of the estate. The stranger claimed he was Robert Kennedy Jr. and that he would very much like to show his children where he had spent so many wonderful vacations. John Castle thought the man resembled a Kennedy but wasn't one hundred percent convinced, so he decided a line of questioning was in order. "'What's the private telephone number of the house?'" Leo remembers Castle asking the visitor, "'Who lived in the carriage house?' And finally what was the name of the man who took care of some of the administrative duties for the family in New York? After searching for the answer the young man replied 'Leo Racine,' and with that Mr. Castle said, 'let him in.'"

*Davidoff Studios secretary Gloria Mosch
and Babe Davidoff in JFK's bedroom.*

The estate that Robert Kennedy Jr. visited was now completely renovated with more than six million dollars of improvements, from air-conditioning to a new addition. Yet despite updating the house into the future, the new owners paid special homage to the past. The palm trees where the Kennedys played football had died, so the Castles studied old photos of the backyard and planted almost identical palms six inches from the original trees. And there beside the tennis court Robert would find the bedroom that his Uncle Jack and his father had shared so many years ago. The room still had its original furniture and was decorated in the customary presidential colors, red, white and blue.

Bob Davidoff donated several of his prints to the John F. Kennedy Library in Boston.

Another young Kennedy, one that Davidoff remembered photographing from the time he was a rambunctious toddler, came to town in 1996. "He was at Trump's Mar-a-Lago Club for a gathering of magazine publishers to represent his new magazine, *George*," recalled Davidoff, who at the time was working as a resident photographer for the club and was on hand to capture the event. It had been many years since Davidoff had seen John F. Kennedy Jr., but the handsome young Kennedy recognized him immediately.

"John, of course, knew me and remembered the photographs of him, his sister and his parents I had taken many years earlier," said Davidoff. "With several photographers trying to get closer, I was the only one allowed to photograph him. That privilege was earned."

Over the years, the Davidoff Studio was frequented by the grandchildren and even great-grandchildren of

Rose and Joe Kennedy. While vacationing in Palm Beach, various Kennedy cousins, including Maria Shriver, would bring their children in to meet the photographer and revisit the many images of their childhood. The treasured photos not only landed in the personal scrapbooks of various Kennedy members but a few iconic photographs of the president and his family now grace the walls of the JFK Library in Boston.

Davidoff always cherished one image of his Kennedy photo archive above the rest. Even after his death in 2004, the picture still hangs in the Davidoff Studio, the one regarded as his favorite. Surprisingly, it is not one of the hundreds of images he took himself over the years. Taken a decade earlier, it shows the photographer standing next to Senator Kennedy and his wife Victoria at a private Palm Beach residence. At the bottom of the photo the senator wrote, To Bob Davidoff, who has photographed all the Kennedys, now working on the next generation."

Gloria Mosch sitting in the library in the Kennedy estate.

Gloria Mosch and Babe Davidoff standing in the staircase of the Kennedy estate. The stone work was very typical of a home designed by Palm Beach architect Addison Mizner.

*The handsome John F. Kennedy Jr.
and his wife, Carolyn Bessette, at
the Mar-a-Lago Club.*

Senator Edward Kennedy and his wife, Victoria, 1995.

Bob Davidoff's cherished Kennedy photograph hangs in the Davidoff Studios in Palm Beach.